A Nap

Consultants

Ashley Bishop, Ed.D.
Sue Bishop, M.E.D.

Publishing Credits

Dona Herweck Rice, *Editor-in-Chief*
Robin Erickson, *Production Director*
Lee Aucoin, *Creative Director*
Tim J. Bradley, *Illustrator Manager*
Chad Thompson, *Illustrator*
Sharon Coan, *Project Manager*
Jamey Acosta, *Editor*
Rachelle Cracchiolo, M.A.Ed., *Publisher*

Teacher Created Materials

5301 Oceanus Drive
Huntington Beach, CA 92649-1030
http://www.tcmpub.com

ISBN 978-1-4333-2927-2

© 2012 Teacher Created Materials, Inc.

cap

I need a cap.

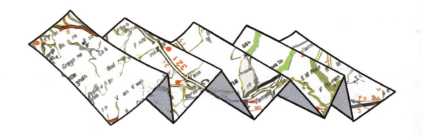

map

I need a map.

tap

I need to tap.

lap

I need a lap.

We need a nap.

Glossary

cap

lap

map

nap

tap

Sight Words

I need
a   to
We

Extension Activities

Read the story together with your child. Use the discussion questions before, during, and after your reading to deepen your child's understanding of the story and the rime (word family) that is introduced.

The activities provide fun ideas for continuing the conversation about the story and the vocabulary that is introduced. They will help your child make personal connections to the story and use the vocabulary to describe prior experiences.

Discussion Questions

- Why do you think the boy put a cap in the suitcase?
- Do you ever wear a cap? When do you wear a cap?
- Each member of the family wants something special for their trip. What do your family members like to bring on trips?
- What activities make you tired and want to take a nap?

Activities at Home

- Review the -ap words in the story. Tell your child to help you clap out the number of words on each page. You can even mention that the word clap is an -ap word, too!
- Have your child sit on your lap. Talk about the -ap words in the story and how you can use them in sentences.

12